# THE EASTER
# ANSWER

## WHAT HAPPENED DURING
## THE FORTY DAYS
## BETWEEN EASTER
## AND THE ASCENSION

### STEPHEN R. KINGSLEY

# THE EASTER ANSWER

Copyright © 2009 by Stephen R. Kingsley

The Easter Answer: What Happened During the Forty Days Between Easter and The Ascension

IBSN 978-1-4276-3671-3
Revised: February 2009

Join the discussion at www.easteranswer.com

Scripture quotations taken from the New American Standard Bible®, Copyright © 1960, 1962, 1963, 1968, 1971, 1972, 1973, 1975, 1977, 1995 by The Lockman Foundation Used by permission. (www.Lockman.org)

PRINTED BY:
BRENTWOOD CHRISTIAN PRESS
COLUMBUS, GEORGIA 31904
www.BrentwoodBooks.com

Special Thanks to the congregations of
the Craigmont Community Church, Craigmont, Idaho and the
Reubens Community Church. Also to the many friends who
have offered their advice and encouragement. Thanks to Kathy
Jackson of Reubens, for layout, formatting, and proofing help.
God bless you.

Dedicated to Paula, Joshua, Charlie, Mason, and Benjamin.

# Table of Contents

# Timeline, Easter to the Ascension

| | | |
|---|---|---|
| *5:45 pm | Mt 28:1 | 2 Marys came to see the tomb. |

**EASTER SUNDAY (BEGAN AT SUNSET) 6:00 PM**

| | | |
|---|---|---|
| Mid.-3am | Mt 28:2-4 | Angel rolls away the stone. |
| 4:00 am to 5:15 am | Jn 20:1-18 Mk 16:9-12 | Mary M. finds stone removed, runs to Peter, the men investigate, Mary 1st to see Jesus, tells the disciples, they don't believe her. |

**EASTER MORNING SUNRISE - 6:00 AM**

| | | |
|---|---|---|
| 6:15 am | Mk 16:1-3 Lk 24:1,2 | Women to tomb, arrive just after sunrise, find stone missing, go in. |
| 6:30 am | Mt 28:5-7 Mk 16:4-6 Lk 24:3-5 | Women enter tomb, see/hear angel seated on right (Mt. & Mk.), and see/hear 2 standing angels. |
| 6:40 am | Mk 16:8 Mt 28:8-10 | Women flee scared speechless, Jesus appears, is worshipped. |
| 6:45 am | Mt 28:11-15 | Soldiers to Priests, take bribes. |
| 7:00 am | Lk 24:9-11 | Women tell others, not believed. |
| 7:10 am | Lk 24:12 | Peter's 2nd sprint to see tomb. |
| Time? | 1 Co 16:5a | Jesus appears to Peter. |
| 9:00 am to 2:00 pm | Mk 16:12 Lk 24:13-32 | Jesus walks w/ 2 men on road to Emmaus. Tells of Messiah. Vanishes after prayer. |

| 5:00 pm | Mk 16:13<br>Lk 24:33-35 | 2 men to Jerusalem. Tell story,<br>they are not believed. |
|---|---|---|

| 5:15 pm | Lk 24:36-49<br>Jn 20:19-25 | 1st appearance of Jesus to group,<br>Thomas not present. |
|---|---|---|

**EIGHT DAYS AFTER EASTER SUNDAY**

| Time ? | Mk 16:14-18<br>Jn 20:26-31<br>1Co 15:5b | 2nd appearance to group, eating,<br>Thomas addressed. Matthias<br>present: "The Twelve (future)" |
|---|---|---|

| Time? | 1Co 15:6 | Jesus appears to over 500 at once. |
|---|---|---|

| Time? | 1Co 15:7a | Jesus appears to his bro. James. |
|---|---|---|

**ABOUT TWO WEEKS AFTER EASTER**

| Morning | Jn 21:1-25 | 3rd to group, Galilee Seashore |
|---|---|---|

**ABOUT THREE WEEKS AFTER EASTER**

| Time? | Mt 28:16-20<br>1Co 15:7b | 4th to group, to "The Eleven"<br>on appointed Mount in Galilee. |
|---|---|---|

**FORTY DAYS AFTER EASTER**

| Time? | Acts 1:1-12<br>Lk 24:50-53<br>Mk 16:19,20 | 5th (and final) appearance to<br>"all the apostles." Jesus ascends<br>in their sight. |
|---|---|---|

**ABOUT TWO YEARS AFTER EASTER**

| Time? | 1Co 18:8 | Jesus appears to Apostle Paul. |
|---|---|---|

Copyright, 2008, Stephen Kingsley, *The Easter Answer*.

* For clarification on the timing of Mt. 28:1 read the book The Easter Answer.

# INTRODUCTION

A STORM OF CONTROVERSY currently surrounds the Bible. An intellectual battle is raging around several questions. Is it inerrant? Is it inspired of God? Is it contradictory? Is it reliable? Was it written when it claims to have been, or after the fact? While Christians are being pressed to answer these questions, they're also struggling to live up to the Book's standards and often falling short. Given the intensity of the conflict both without and within, some have fled the faith and are now trying to persuade others to do the same.

Decades ago, there was a young and talented Christian filled with a zeal for evangelism. Being gifted in music he wrote several popular Christian songs, including many for children. Eventually he ended up in ministry, serving as a pastor. But doubts began to set in concerning the Bible and Christianity and this gifted young man lost his God and his faith. But he didn't just turn away from faith towards some other line of interest; he became a celebrity for atheism. He's the co-president of an organization of around 13,000 atheists that is, among other things, engaged in numerous legal battles. They would like to remove all references to God and expressions of religious faith from government and public life. His name is Dan Barker of the Freedom From Religion Foundation (FFRF) based out of Madison, Wisconsin. You may not remember hearing the name of Barker's organization, but if you read newspapers or watch the news on TV, you've heard about them. In 1994 FFRF sued the U.S. federal government in an effort to have "In God We Trust" removed as the national motto. The case went before the Supreme Court in 1996, the judges decided not to rule on it. Among other cases, they filed suit recently against President Bush and the U.S. government for declaring a National Day of Prayer. In various cities across the nation, they continue to challenge such things as monuments that include the posting of the Ten Commandments and nativity scenes in parks and on courthouse lawns. They've also begun an advertising campaign that includes a recent full-page ad in the *New York Times* inviting others to join their cause. And they've purchased billboards in several major cities. Most recently, in December of '08, Barker placed an atheist sign next to a nativity scene in the Washington State Capitol building, something that caused quite a stir. Bill O'Reilly of Fox News reported on it several times during the Christmas season.

After joining FFRF, Inc. as public relations director Barker wrote a book titled *Losing Faith in Faith* [1992, FFRF, Inc., Madison, Wisconsin] to chronicle his journey into atheism. Not only does Barker aim to explain, but his book is written to snag Christians by giving them reasons to abandon their faith and join him in the free and happy world of atheism. Among his devices is a long list of Bible absurdities and contradictions. Within that list is one which has become known as The Easter Challenge. Barker's Challenge is aimed at demonstrating that the Bible accounts of Christ's resurrection and subsequent appearances are contradictory, and therefore unreliable. Since the whole of Christianity rises and falls on the merits of the claim of Christ's resurrection from the dead, Barker's Easter Challenge is intended to pierce the heart of the Christian faith with a deadly wound. Barker makes his challenge and expounds upon the alleged resurrection discrepancies in his *Losing Faith* book in a chapter titled "Leave No Stone Unturned." The following is taken from the opening of this chapter and lays out the specific criteria of the challenge (used with permission):

> I have an Easter challenge for Christians. My challenge is simply this: tell me what happened on Easter. I am not asking for proof. My straightforward request is merely that Christians tell me exactly what happened on the day that their most important doctrine was born.

Believers should eagerly take up this challenge, since without the resurrection, there is no Christianity. Paul wrote, "And if Christ be not risen, then is our preaching vain, and your faith is also vain. Yea, and we are found false witnesses of God; because we have testified of God that he raised up Christ: whom he raised not up, if so be that the dead rise not." (I Corinthians 15:14-15)

The conditions of the challenge are simple and reasonable. In each of the four Gospels, begin at Easter morning and read to the end of the book: Matthew 28, Mark 16, Luke 24, and John 20-21. Also read Acts 1:3-12 and Paul's tiny version of the story in I Corinthians 15:3-8. These 165 verses can be read in a few moments. Then, without omitting a single detail from these separate accounts, write a simple, chronological narrative of the events between the resurrection and the ascension: what happened first, second, and so on; who said what, when; and where these things happened.

Since the gospels do not always give precise times of day, it is permissible to make educated guesses. The narrative does not have to pretend to present a perfect picture—it only needs to give at least one plausible account of all of the facts. Additional explanation of the narrative may be set apart in parentheses. The important condition to the challenge, however, is that not one single biblical detail be omitted. Fair enough?

I have tried this challenge myself. I failed. An Assembly of God minister whom I was debating a couple of years ago on a Florida radio show loudly proclaimed over the air that he would send me the narrative in a few days. I am still waiting. After my debate at the University of Wisconsin, "Jesus of Nazareth: Messiah or Myth," a Lutheran graduate student told me he accepted the challenge and would be contacting me in about a week. I have never heard from him. Both of these people, and others, agreed that the request was reasonable and crucial. Maybe they are slow readers.

Being confident that I've met Barker's terms and have successfully answered his Challenge, I mailed my solution to him in February of 2008. He hasn't answered yet. Maybe he's a "slow reader" too? Not likely. Barker is a member of the Prometheus Society, a very exclusive high-IQ club of less than one hundred members. According to their website: "Membership in the society is open to anyone who has received a score on an accepted IQ test that is equal to or greater than that received by the highest one thirty-thousandth of the general population[1]." Barker is a very smart guy.

I can't help but wonder if he hasn't responded because maybe, just maybe, he cannot find a contradiction in my answer to his Challenge. If that's so, then Barker is in a very awkward position. He has enjoyed challenging Christians on this supposed Bible flaw for years and boasted widely over our failure to respond. If indeed I've been true to the text of the Bible and put the accounts together without a valid contradiction will he be able to acknowledge it? Perhaps Barker is now the one facing a challenge. Maybe? After waiting over six months to hear from him, I sent an email to Barker asking him to reply to my answer to his Easter Challenge. Though he says he's very busy promoting his new book (September 2008) *godless: How an Evangelical Preacher Became One of America's Leading Atheists* (complete with forward by Richard Dawkins), he promised he would get around to responding. In the meantime, you can review my solution for yourself in this book and make your own decision on the merits of my claim. The accusation of contradiction is serious and deserves our thoughtful consideration and if possible, a convincing apologetic.

Lest you think you're reading a book written by a scholar, I should tell you up front that I'm not one. I'm just a small town pastor. In 1975 I graduated from Lewiston High School (Idaho) with about a C average. And I have an Associate's degree from a small non-accredited Bible school that no longer exists. I'm writing as nothing more than a Bible reader and lover. But perhaps knowing that will make this booklet more interesting for you. I hope so. Dan Barker's Challenge was made to "Christians." I can claim to be one. And if, as you read this you find yourself thinking, "This really makes sense," then you'll know why I felt compelled to write it. It makes sense to me too. So, bear with me if you find I failed to follow proper academic protocols. It's not intentional. *The Easter Answer* is intended as only a brief overview of the problem and to present an outline of what I see as a solution, a relatively simple one from a simple man.

The main part of this book, the narrative of what happened between Easter and the ascension, is a story about a profound happening and the struggle of a host of interesting characters to come to grips with its meaning. But it's more than a story; allegedly, it is historical fact. That's the real question, maybe history's greatest question: Did Jesus really, literally, rise from the dead? For that reason, these Bible accounts by five writers of what happened on Easter and the forty days that followed deserve our attention. Important questions should be answered with care.

By the time we're done, I hope you'll agree that the accounts are consistent, not contradictory. But even if the light doesn't come on for you, even if you don't think the resurrection narratives have been or can be harmonized, their historical significance as evidence to explain Christianity can not be easily dismissed. I only hope to add these thoughts to the discussion and see what comes of it. And I hope you'll join the discussion and express your opinion on this book's success or failure. Go to www.easteranswer.com and click on "Cast Your Vote." Let's begin.


Stephen Kingsley
Craigmont, Idaho

# Chapter One

# THE EASTER CHALLENGE

ACCORDING TO DAN BARKER, in the sixteen years since he published his Easter Challenge, very few Christians have responded. Of those who have, none have been able to write "a simple, chronological narrative of the events between the resurrection and the ascension." Others who share Barker's perspective have picked up on this perceived weakness in Christian doctrine and have made similar challenges of their own. I was made aware of the Easter Challenge in April of 2003 when a skeptic from a neighboring town published his own abbreviated version of the Challenge in our regional newspaper. This man went so far as to offer a reward to anyone who could answer successfully.

Easter Challenge[2]

Once again Easter is upon us. Now go to your Bible and put together the various Resurrection stories into one consistent narrative. Read Matthew 28, Mark 16, Luke 24 and John 20 & 21. Read also Acts 1:3–12 and 1 Corinthians 15:3–8. List all the events from the Resurrection to the Ascension of Jesus without omitting any detail.

If you can do this with no contradictions I will pay you a $1,000 reward. Mail your claim to Resurrection Reward, [address omitted[3]] If you have email, send it to nielsen@uidaho.edu. Read the Bible carefully. Thank you.

Ralph Nielsen, Moscow

Like many Christians, I assumed the Challenge would be easy to answer. Why wouldn't it be? And being a pastor within the geographical area Nielsen targeted, I felt an obligation to answer. His Challenge seems innocent enough, but he's certain his $1000 is safe. He baited his hook to catch a few Christians, but I think he's been snagged by it himself. Because Nielsen added a promise to pay for services rendered (which I'm claiming to have provided) it seems he has obligated himself to a reasonable standard of fairness. I doubt a court would be willing to decide the case, but it should be put before the court of public opinion--one of the reasons I've written this book. If you end up thinking Nielsen owes me a $1,000, please don't give him a hard time about it. He's a nice guy (even if spiritually blind) and never imagined anyone would ever come close to a successful answer.

As I began working on this, I wrote to several top Christian scholars and asked them how the apparent contradictions in the resurrection accounts were handled on the academic level. I was favored with several replies from which I learned that the problem is pervasive and widely acknowledged. Dr. Daniel Wallace of Dallas Theological Seminary replied, "No plausible solution has presented itself." Others agree. Dr. J. Lyle Story of Regent University apprised me of the current view of scholars saying, "I do know that it's next to impossible to provide the sequence of events in the post-Resurrections. . .there's no way that they can all be harmonized." Dr. Donald Hagner of Fuller Theological Seminary in Dallas calls the problem of reconciling the resurrection narratives a "notorious" one.

While many Christian scholars see the accounts as impossible to reconcile, skeptics and atheists like Dan Barker take it a step further, claiming the accounts are contradictory; some even go so far as to suggest only fools could possibly believe the resurrection was a real, historical event. An example of such rhetoric is found in an article titled "The Resurrection Maze" by Farrell Till, editor of the *Skeptical Review*, a journal of biblical criticism.

Juxtaposed and considered as a single story, the four resurrection accounts form a veritable maze of contradictions. So once again I must remind readers of the rule of evidence that says *falsus in uno, falsus in omnibus* (false in one thing, false in everything). When alleged witnesses to an event contradict themselves as flagrantly as did the four gospel writers in their accounts of the resurrection, everything that they said must be viewed with suspicion. These writers claimed that a man who was physically dead returned to life. A claim that extraordinary requires extraordinary proof, but there is certainly nothing extraordinary in the resurrection testimony of Matthew, Mark, Luke, and John. It is so riddled with inconsistencies that no one but the hopelessly credulous could possibly believe it... If Matthew, Mark, Luke, and John—all four of them—had really been guided and directed by an omniscient, omnipotent deity while they were writing their gospels (as the inerrancy doctrine claims), there would be no maze of inconsistencies in the juxtaposition of their stories. There would be that perfect unity and harmony that fundamentalist preachers talk about so much—but which doesn't really exist. I'm very afraid that the faith of Christians who have put so much hope in the resurrection will prove to be vain and that they will, unfortunately, never know that "they are of all men most miserable[4].

At the heart of this issue is the biblical evidence of the stories which were written of the events surrounding Christianity's claim that Christ was literally resurrected from the dead, was seen alive, and ascended into heaven. Consistency, if indeed it is granted to exist, doesn't prove the resurrection happened or that the writers were "guided and directed by an omniscient, omnipotent deity while they were writing their gospels," but it certainly shows that the biblical evidence God has provided us today is far more reliable than critics like Till have wanted us to believe.

When the Pharisees demanded a sign of Jesus, he replied by saying the only sign he would give them was his resurrection from the dead (Mt. 12:38-40). Yet no one saw the resurrection happen. How then was the sign given? While some were eyewitnesses of Christ alive from the dead, wounds and all, Christianity grew on the winds of nothing more than the testimony of witnesses accompanied by the historical narrative of the Old Testament scriptures concerning the Messiah. While the witnesses themselves were given the direct, objective evidence of seeing and handling the resurrected body of Jesus, the Pharisees to whom Jesus promised the sign were only given the second-hand (or even further removed) testimony of the witnesses. But according to the historical record in Acts, for many of the Jewish hierarchy, this circumstantial evidence of his sign was enough: "The word of God kept on spreading; and the number of the disciples continued to increase greatly in Jerusalem, and a great many of the priests were becoming obedient to the faith (Acts 6:7)." Many others accepted the circumstantial evidence of second- or third-hand testimony, and Christianity spread.

Today, explanations of conspiracy and deliberate deception have been offered to account for the rise of first-century Christianity, but for many, the most plausible explanation is that Jesus really did rise from the dead. This belief today is not without historical support. For example, Christianity grew so quickly from Jerusalem that by the time Rome burned in 64 AD there were enough Christians in Rome for Nero to try to convince his subjects that they had started the fires. Looking for a scapegoat, would Nero try to blame the fires on a group no one had heard of? The implication, based on history, is that in little more than thirty years after the time of Jesus most citizens in Rome knew about Christianity. It's unlikely that the early faith could have grown so quickly unless it were spread by those who had reason to be convinced and were willing to suffer for their cause. In addition to numerous non-biblical historical references and sources for early Christianity, best of all we have the direct written testimony handed down to us through the ages of perhaps four eyewitnesses (the Gospels bearing the names of Matthew and John, the testimony of Paul, and the resurrection affirmations found in 1 Peter), plus the second-hand written reports penned by the writers of Mark and Luke. These accounts were written within a few decades of Jesus' death to narrate his life and resurrection while many of the original witnesses were still alive and could affirm them. If indeed the resurrection accounts are accurate portrayals of real events, even though partial, it's reasonable to expect that they somehow fit together without undue strain. Barker's Easter Challenge is indeed crucial and his conditions fairly stated.

I sent my solution to Nielsen and we had an enjoyable email debate over the merits of my claim. Though he didn't limit his version of the Challenge to the use of a specific Bible version, he denied my claim to his $1000 reward saying I had used an "out of step," "mistranslated," and "obscure" version of the Bible. Which? The American Standard Version of 1901, the Bible which indeed was the standard in many U.S. seminaries through most of the twentieth century. More on Bible versions in an upcoming chapter, including a close look at the key verse which was central to Nielsen's denial of my claim, the verse he says was mistranslated. When this verse is understood it provides a new point of reference from which to order the particulars of what happened on the day the Christian faith was born.

The Easter Challenge has been widely published and its impact felt. It has bolstered the confidence of atheists, skeptics, and antagonists. Many of them think this battle is over, and in this matter Christians have conceded defeat. The following is a comment by atheist writer Francois Tremblay about the failure of Christians to produce an answer to the Easter Challenge:

Given that all we have is an incoherent account, coupled with the fact that it is in a religiously-motivated, non-contemporary book, failure to answer to the Challenge is little more than the last nail in the cross (so to speak). That Christians rely on such a silly story for the center of their faith is a testimony to the paucity of evidence for the Christian worldview, and religious worldviews in general[5].

Perhaps Tremblay pronounced his judgment of "failure" too soon.

If the accounts are consistent, then they always have been. It's simply a matter of carefully examining the texts, granting the words the meaning the writers most likely intended, and adjusting our viewpoint accordingly as the accounts are added to one another to form one narrative.

Maybe it's time for a resurrection of the resurrection accounts.

Chapter Two
# LOGISTICS AND OBSERVATIONS

IN UNDERTAKING THE TASK of reconciling the resurrection accounts, it is necessary to clarify the goal. The issue at hand concerns nothing more than the contradiction and/or consistency of the accounts penned by the various writers, not whether the resurrection really happened. In debating the merits of my claim with Ralph Nielsen, the issue of historicity was raised as a potential disqualifier. I responded, "Had your public challenge been to list the sequence of events in *Gulliver's Travels* without contradiction, the sequencing would be the issue, not how it was that little human Lilliputians could come to exist and tie up a man twelve times their size with their tiny ropes. Please, let's stick to the substance of your challenge." The accounts contain records of supernatural events such as the appearances of angels to the natural eyes of the women, the resurrection of a man from the dead, and his appearances after the fact, including his showing up in the midst of a closed room. Even if the accounts are assumed fictional, it's yet possible to fairly judge the consistency of the writings.

## FRAGMENTS AND SIMPLE ADDITION

If each Gospel was rigidly bound as an indivisible whole, and a rule made and enforced that required each to be taken as its own complete story, it might be possible to convict the accounts of contradiction. When so considered and given only a side-by-side comparison, they certainly seem to be in conflict in numerous places. For example, if it were required that Luke's Gospel be taken as a full and complete story, the reader would naturally conclude that after Jesus appeared to his brethren and spoke to them on the afternoon of Easter, he then led them out to Bethany and ascended that same afternoon. During the appearance of Jesus to the group of disciples on Easter Sunday afternoon, Luke records the speech he gave and then follows in vss. 50 and 51 with, "And He led them out as far as Bethany. . .and was carried up into heaven." If we then compare Luke's ascension story to that found in Acts, we have a problem. In Acts 1:3 it is plainly stated that Jesus was seen of his disciples over a period of forty days before being taken up into heaven. Critics frequently assert these two records are contradictory concerning when the ascension happened. But are they really?

To prove contradiction in this case (and numerous others in the resurrection accounts) critics must prove the existence of a rule that prevents the Gospels from being added together to form a more complete picture. Had Luke, in vs. 50 wrote, "and *that same day* he led them out to Bethany. . ." then contradiction could be proved. But, in Luke, the writer did not specify *when* the ascension happened, only that it did. For the when, we need only turn to Acts 1:3 and add its information to that learned by reading Luke. It's a common function of the mind to assume one thing based on a limited view and then make adjustments as more information is added. It would be ludicrous to argue for the imposition of such a rule in the case of the resurrection accounts when such a thing would be forbidden in all other learning situations. The accounts prove one another incomplete, not contradictory. They are only partial records of what happened, not seamless flowing narratives. Each provides pieces of the same story: the quest in this writing being to demonstrate that they can be added to one another in a complimentary way without strain or conflict.

## THE REQUIRED APPROACH TO THE PROBLEM

Our method then requires us to identify each event clearly in each account, separate it from its native source, and subject it to the influence of the other pieces. Once the pieces are distinguished, it's simply a matter of determining where each belongs in the chronology. And finally, we need only add the information in the pieces together to form a narrative which provides a more complete picture.

Our task is one of logic and good sense. For the result to be convincing, it is reasonable to expect the natural sequential chronology of each account to be preserved in the newly formed end narrative.

## CAREFUL DISCERNMENT IS NEEDED

When evaluating statements in the resurrection accounts it is important to determine if the things being described and compared are similar or identical. If I burned a log in my fireplace Monday morning and then burned another on Tuesday morning, the logs are similar, not identical. The logs looked the same and met the same fate in the same way, but they weren't identical. Logically, it would be impossible to burn the same (identical) log on both days. This is an important distinction in our study. For example, different Gospel writers tell of women going to the tomb. One of the reasons the accounts have seemed impossible to reconcile is our assumption that the Evangelists were all writing about the identical trip at the same time. When we watch the details carefully it may be proved differently. Often, the very details which have given critics reason to criticize the accounts are the very details which provide the justification to distinguish the events as similar and supplemental rather than identical and contradictory.

## UNDERSTANDING CONTRADICTION

Consistency is granted among things that can be demonstrated to agree. Contradiction is its opposite. The main version of Aristotle's famous law of non-contradiction states, "It is impossible for the same thing to belong and not to belong at the same time to the same thing and in the same respect." Modern definitions follow the same line of logic. If it can be proved that statements are indeed about the same thing at the same time and in the same respect, then it's simply a matter of determining if the alleged truth of one statement makes the alleged truth of the other a logical impossibility. If so, contradiction has been proved to exist. But if not, then the statements must be accepted as consistent, even though it must be understood that consistency in and of itself doesn't prove that the statements are true.

Contradiction is a serious accusation against written statements. If it can be established with certainty, it proves that one of the statements is certainly false, at least in part. If one is false, the others might be too. If several are proved false, there is good reason to doubt what is being claimed. Because an accusation of contradiction is so potentially destructive, it should be made with caution, and hastily withdrawn if disproved.

## GIVING THE CHALLENGER WHAT HE ASKED FOR

When the fragmentary nature of the accounts is properly noted, the method of bringing the various pieces together into one new narrative is justified. It should be observed that this is exactly what Barker asked for when he wrote his Easter Challenge. Had he restricted the solver to only a juxtaposition of the accounts, keeping them apart with each bound to the limited view that the events naturally flowed along a continuous timeline, his Challenge would be impossible to champion. But Barker said, "without omitting a single detail from these separate accounts, write a simple, chronological narrative of the events between the resurrection and the ascension: what happened first, second, and so on; who said what, when; and where these things happened. Since the gospels do not always give precise times of day, it is permissible to make educated guesses. The narrative does not have to pretend to present a perfect picture—it only needs to give at least one plausible account of all of the facts." Clearly Baker expects the solver to create one narrative ("a...narrative" and "the narrative" and "one...account") from the details of the separate narratives which he identified and specified. It is true that when the accounts are kept separate from one another and compared, they appear contradictory—that's a given. But Barker's Challenge is not about keeping the accounts apart from one another and trying to explain away the apparent problems as if dealing with different stories. By requiring the solver to make one list of the events in "a narrative" he has licensed the appropriate method by which to test the appearances of contradiction to see if they may be validated. That's the challenge of the Easter Challenge. Barker's present challenge (and Nielsen's) is to examine this solution and document any place in the narrative where a contradiction may be logically proved. Barker made the rules when he published the Challenge, he should judge by them. He can not criticize the method of making one narrative.

# Chapter Three

# A GOOD BEGINNING

IN ADDITION TO THE BASIC approach to reconciliation outlined in the previous chapter, an important clarification in one verse of Scripture must be acknowledged. The solving of the Challenge begins with Matthew 28:1 which gives two important back-to-back temporal (time indicating) phrases. Here is Mt. 28:1 from the 1995 Updated New American Standard Bible (U-NASB):

> (Matthew 28:1) Now <u>after</u> the Sabbath, as it began to dawn toward the first *day* of the week, Mary Magdalene and the other Mary came to look at the grave. [underlining mine for emphasis]

According to Matthew, the two Marys went "to look at the grave." I'd like to give careful consideration to *when* they went. Let's take the two temporal phrases of Mt. 28:1 one at a time, considering each in turn. We'll begin with the first, "Now after the Sabbath," and then the second "as it began to dawn toward the first day of the week." The solution to reconciling the resurrection accounts begins with understanding these two temporal phrases in the way the original writer most likely intended.

The U-NASB version of the Bible is a favorite among scholars because of the literalness of its translation from the original Greek to English. However, the problem presented in the translation of Mt. 28:1 is readily apparent when comparing the 1995 U-NASB passage to the NASB as it was originally published when it first came on the market in 1971:

> (Matthew 28:1) Now <u>late</u> on the Sabbath, as it began to dawn toward the first *day* of the week, Mary Magdalene

and the other Mary came to look at the grave. [underlining mine for emphasis]

As seen by comparing Mt. 28:1 in the original NASB of '71 to the Updated NASB of '95 above, the phrase "late on the Sabbath" was changed to "after the Sabbath." The Greek word at issue here is *opse*. This seemingly small textual change in the phrase *opse de sabbatôn* makes for a major difference in the time of day being described. Even a cursory examination of the Jewish method of timekeeping reveals that Jewish days switched from one to the next with the setting of the sun. Orthodox Jews today still use the same reckoning. Knowing that, "late on the Sabbath" must be acknowledged as a reference to the time of day near the end of the Sabbath when the sun was nearing the horizon, about to set. But, "*after* the Sabbath" could mean any time after the Sabbath day was over.

The "after the Sabbath" translation has been readily accepted. First, it presents no difficulty with the description in both Mark 16 and Luke 24 of the women going to the tomb with spices on Easter morning and arriving just after sunrise. Commonly, we have assumed Mt. 28:1 to be a description of the beginning of this Easter morning trip by the women to the tomb. The "after the Sabbath" translation seems preferable because it fits with our understanding of what we know about the timing of the resurrection and the trip by the women on Easter morning to spice the body of Jesus. But, remember too that many experts concede the resurrection accounts have never been reconciled in a plausible way, so let's make sure the older translation of "late on the Sabbath" deserves to be discarded.

It is only as of late that a plethora of English Bibles have emerged that have provided "after the Sabbath" for the first temporal phrase of Mt. 28:1. A survey of English Bibles reveals that historically, this first phrase has been translated as either "late on the Sabbath [ASV, NASB (originally), et al]," "in the end of the Sabbath [KJV, et al]," and in ancient English Bibles as "in the evening of the Sabbath [Cloverdale, et al]."

# THE PUBLISHER SPEAKS

Upon discovering the change in the NASB translation of Greek *opse*, Mt. 28:1, from "late on the Sabbath" to "after the Sabbath," I was eager to know how the change had been justified. To their credit, the Lockman Foundation, owners of the NASB, maintain an editorial board to answer such questions. I wrote and asked them why they had done so and received the following reply (used by permission):

This decision was made in the earlier history of the NASB, before the '95 Update. The primary argument for the original choice of "late" is that it is the usual meaning for the Greek word in question ("*opse*"), and the meaning "after" is not attested for in Greek literature until the second century. Matt. 28:1 is the only verse in the New Testament which seems to require "after" as the meaning for the word. So the original translators were hard-pressed to justify "after" as the translation, even though the lexicons provide it for this verse, and instead they explored ways in which "late" could be understood that were consistent with the other gospel accounts. There were some possibilities: 1) Matthew is not speaking of the usual sundown-to-sundown Jewish day but of a sunrise-to-sunrise day, so that in this case "Sabbath" includes the hours before 6 AM Sunday; 2) The Greek "*opse*" corresponds to the rabbinic concept of the "exit" of a day, so Matthew is using the Greek equivalent of their term for Saturday night; 3) according to a tenth-century Greek lexicon by Suda, the Greek for "Sabbath" in this case means "week," not the Sabbath day, so Matthew is referring to the end of the week, i.e. Saturday night going into Sunday.

The later decision for "after" came as a result of ruling out explanations for "late" and reconsidering the recommendations of the lexicons. As to the possibilities stated above, #1 finds support in the fact that Matthew does seem to be using the sunrise-to-sunrise accounting when he says that "it began to dawn toward the first day. . ." But it is very unlikely that a Jew, even one in a profession of low social standing, would speak of the Sabbath itself this loosely. Even within a sunrise-to-sunrise reckoning of the week it is far more likely that he would mean the usual sunset-to-sunset understanding of the Sabbath. In his own business dealings he would constantly be reminded of the fact. The weakness of #2 is that "late" does not really correspond to "exit," and to argue that it does simply leads to the equivalent of "after." As for #3, it is true that the word in Matt 28:1 for Sabbath ("sabbaton" in plural) is the same as the word for "week," and in fact this same word is used a little later in the verse where it clearly means "week" (literally "first of sabbaton"). One could argue that the same word in the same verse most likely has the same meaning throughout. But there are problems, e.g. "late in the week" would seem to refer to the final day or days of the week rather than to Saturday night, as the tenth-century lexicon maintains, and it is odd that Matthew would use such a general term after being specific earlier in his account of passion week (cf. Matt. 27:62). Also, the combination of "late in the week" followed by "toward the first day of the week" is awkward, as it relies upon the reader's inference that these are two consecutive weeks. On the other hand, the standard lexicons, including the unabridged LSJM for Classical Greek, all acknowledge the possibility of "after" for the verse, and the second-century citations are close enough in time to indicate that this could have been an accepted meaning when the gospels were written.

The above reveals the subjective nature of the decision made by the NASB translators for their change of "late in the Sabbath" in Mt. 28:1 to "after the Sabbath." Judging by their stated reasons for making the change, nothing in the original text demanded them to do so. They begin their explanation with this statement: "Matt. 28:1 is the only verse in the New Testament which seems to require 'after' as the meaning for the word." They did not explain why it "seems" to require a change. Is it the emergence of "after" in other newer versions? Is it Markan influence of "When the Sabbath was over (16:1)?" Were they hoping to make the first phrase consistent with "dawn" in the second? It may have been a combination of these pressures. Be that as it may, judging by their explanation the change seems thinly justified, if warranted at all.

## THE SECOND TEMPORAL PHRASE

When it comes to the second phrase, there is no conflict regarding translation. It is almost always provided in exactly the same way in every English Bible as, "as it began to dawn toward the first *day* of the week." If we grant that the writer intended to describe the time of day in the first phrase as "late on the Sabbath," the second phrase initially appears contradictory because we immediately assume the word "dawn" to be a reference to the approach of daylight on Easter morning. While this seems obvious, especially considering the influence brought to bear by Mark and Luke's descriptions of the women arriving at the tomb just after sunrise on Easter morning, we must delve deeper. It is doubtful that the writer intentionally and blatantly contradicted himself by describing just before sunset on the Sabbath in the first phrase and just before sunrise on the first day of the week (Easter Sunday) in the second.

In Mt. 28:1, the five words translated "as it began to dawn" is the Greek active participle *epiphoskouse*, which means "dawning." The question which must be asked is what exactly is "dawning" and when? The same Greek word has only one other New Testament usage, which is used in a temporal phrase in much the same way. Remarkably it is used of the burial of Jesus, specifically to indicate the time of day that he was buried. Luke makes plain that Jesus died at about the ninth hour of the day, corresponding to our 3:00 p.m. That same day he was hastily buried. Lk. 23 narrates his burial and then states in verse 54: "It was the preparation day, and the Sabbath was about to begin." The words "was about to begin" are the Greek verb *epiphosko*. Clearly, Jesus was buried late in the afternoon of the preparation day (Friday) as the Jewish Sabbath "was about to begin" (*epiphosko*) at sunset. If, in Mt. 28:1, *epiphosko* is allowed to have the same influence on its subject, "the first day of the week" as it does on its subject "the Sabbath" in Lk. 23:54, we must then conclude that the second temporal phrase of Mt. 28:1 is referring to the same time of day as in Lk. 23:54, just before sunset.

## THE DAWN OF A NEW DAY AT SUNSET

Now let's return to the first temporal phrase of Mt. 28:1 and consider both together. If then *opse* is translated as "late on the Sabbath," as seems to be the most obvious translation, and knowing the meaning of *epiphosko* in the second phrase, no conflict need exist between both back-to-back temporal phrases of Mt. 28:1. Even in English the phrase "as it began to dawn toward the first day of the week" can be seen as consistent with "late on the Sabbath." It need only be understood that "dawn" here is a reference to the rise of the new 24 hour day, the first day of the week, which was about to commence with the setting of the Sun on the Sabbath. In English, "dawn" is used to describe the rise of any new thing and is often used in conjunction with the rise of a specific period of time, as in "the dawn of a new era." I used to be a radio deejay and worked the midnight to 6:00 a.m. shift at KOZE in Lewiston, Idaho. I would often open my show at midnight saying, "Welcome to the dawn of a new day." No one ever corrected me by insisting the day didn't dawn until sunrise. My meaning was understood by all.

Many newer versions have followed suit with the 1995 Updated NASB in translating *opse* as "after" in Mt. 28:1, including the popular New King James Version and the New International Version. But, it should be noted that neither Barker nor Nielsen limited Challenge respondents to a specific Bible version. It seems dishonest to add qualifications and limitations to a widely publicized challenge long after the fact in order to disqualify a successful answer. In my debate with Nielsen he dogmatically refused to acknowledge any other meaning for "dawn" than the approach of daylight. It's yet to see if Barker will acknowledge the reasonableness of both the Greek and the English sense of the phrases in Mt. 28:1. As Barker stated, "The narrative does not have to pretend to present a perfect picture — it only needs to give at least one plausible account of all of the facts." It would be inconsistent with his expressed standard of fairness to now require a solver to disprove all other possibilities in addition to presenting the merits of the one he's arguing for. At a minimum, my position on Mt. 28:1 is supported by various translations and dictionaries. Though it isn't the only possible view of Mt. 28:1 and it isn't absolute, my position on Mt. 28:1 is plausible.

It seems the writer of Matthew went to great lengths with two phrases to let the reader know that on the evening of the Sabbath, as it began to dawn toward the first day of the week (the 24-hour day which began at sunset) Mary Magdalene and the other Mary came to see the tomb where Jesus was buried. By so doing Matthew is establishing the fact that at the end of the weekly Sabbath, the two anxious women looked upon the tomb; and absent any alarm being raised during this Sabbath evening visit, we're to know the two Marys found everything as expected and returned home. In this way the writer of Matthew establishes the concern of the women and lets his readers know that the stone was in place over the opening to the tomb as the Sabbath ended. Hence, the scene was set and the stage dressed for the dawning of history's most important day.

There is one further piece of supporting evidence in favor of the view that Mt. 28:1 is a reference to a unique and independent trip taken by the women to see the tomb on Sabbath evening.

Unlike the accounts of the sunrise Sunday morning trip of the women in Mk. 16:1,2 and Lk. 24:1-3, the record of Mt. 28:1 makes no mention of their intention of spicing the body of Jesus. In Matthew they simply went "to see" the tomb.

Chapter Four
# A BASKET OF EASTER GOODIES

WE BEGIN NOW the careful work of assembling a step-by-step narrative through all the verses of Scripture that cover the resurrection of Jesus and the chronology of the events that led up to his ascension into heaven. I've broken the forty-day narrative into several chapters so that it will be easier to process, but please consider it as one. This chapter begins with the trip by the two Marys to see the tomb late on the Sabbath day and ends before sunrise on Easter morning.

In the narrative of the forty days between the resurrection of Jesus and the ascension in the five chapters that follow, the New American Standard Bible, copyrighted 1971 has been used. It is nearly identical to the Updated NASB of '95 except, most notably, concerning the word "late" in Mt. 28:1 as opposed to the '95 version's "after." When I originally answered both Nielsen and Barker I wasn't aware that the NASB version originally featured "late" for the Greek *opse* in Mt. 28:1. Had I known, it would have been my preference over the ASV of 1901. The NASB is more recent and, lacking the King's English, better suited to the modern reader. Though I have not checked all Bible versions, I have applied the solution herein to many. I'm glad to report that in all that I've checked (allowing for variations of Mt. 28:1) it works fine. Of all 165 verses covering Easter to the ascension, I see no reason why this arrangement would not work easily in any faithfully translated Bible in any language.

According to Barker's allowance, I've made my educated guesses using our modern 24-hour clock and put them in brackets. I'm not suggesting they are absolute. They are consistent with the temporal references in the texts and offered to show the plausibility of the chronology, allowing plenty of time for the characters to do what is stated or implied.

Each event is listed in order, followed by the scripture that supports it, and then any necessary clarification follows and is set in parentheses. Each chapter ends with a summary in which I take the liberty of adding a few embellishments.

**Event 1.)** *[Time: About an hour before sunset on the Sabbath, Saturday evening]* **Near the end of the weekly Sabbath, just before sundown, the two grieving Marys came together to look upon the tomb where Jesus was buried. They looked upon it and returned home.**

Mt. 28:1 Now late on the Sabbath, as it began to dawn toward the first *day* of the week, Mary Magdalene and the other Mary came to look at the grave.

**Event 2.)** *[Time: In the early morning, perhaps between midnight and 3:00 a.m., the first day of the week, i.e. Easter Sunday]* **A great earthquake occurred around the site of the tomb of Jesus. The angel of the Lord descended from heaven and rolled away the stone that covered the opening of the tomb, then sat on it. In fear of the angel, the Roman soldiers who were guarding the tomb passed out.**

Mt. 28:2 And behold, a severe earthquake had occurred, for an angel of the Lord descended from heaven and came and rolled away the stone and sat upon it.
Mt. 28:3 And his appearance was like lightning, and his garment as white as snow;
Mt. 28:4 and the guards shook for fear of him, and became like dead men.

(Based on a correct understanding of the temporal phrases of Mt. 28:1 some Bible students take the position that the resurrection happened on the evening of the Sabbath, but this is unlikely for several reasons. There is no tradition to support such a claim. And Mk. 16:9 plainly states, "Jesus was risen early the first day

39

of the week." Proponents of the Saturday afternoon resurrection theory believe Jesus died and was buried on Wednesday afternoon. But that does not square with the reckoning of the Emmaus witnesses who said, "besides all this, it is now the third day since these things came to pass (Lk. 24:21)." Had Jesus been crucified on Wednesday, by the common reckoning of that day the witnesses would have said it was the fifth day since these things (the crucifixion of Jesus), not the third.

Jewish reckoning allows that part of a day could count for a full day. Jesus died on Friday afternoon, was in the grave the full 24 hours of the Sabbath, and rose "the third day[6]." Pinning the angel's rolling away of the stone to the resurrection event between midnight and 3:00 a.m. covers the "early the first day of the week" of Mk. 16:9 and puts the event far enough into the first day of the week to qualify for reckoning it as a day, i.e, "the third day." Clearly there is reason to allow for the existence of a gap of time between the Sabbath evening trip of the two Marys "to see" the tomb and the appearance of the angel who rolled away the stone.)

**Event 3.)** *[Time: Around 4:00 a.m., the first day of the week, Easter Sunday]* **Mary Magdalene ventured out to look upon the tomb yet again. She came "early...while it was yet dark" and was alarmed to discover that the stone was missing from the opening to the tomb.**

Jn. 20:1 Now on the first *day* of the week Mary Magdalene came early to the tomb, while it was still dark, and saw the stone *already* taken away from the tomb.

(One of the principle difficulties under the traditional model of a sunrise resurrection event has been trying to fit John's account of Mary Magdalene together with her activities in the Synoptics [Matthew, Mark, and Luke].

Nearly all attempts at harmonization portray Mary as leaving the other women at some point. Such models seem strained because she certainly seems present with the other women throughout their experiences. The advantage of the proposed solution of this book is evident. In this model all Mary's experiences in John commence "early (on the first day of the week) while it was still dark (around 4:00 a.m.)." From this viewpoint, Mary does all these things in Jn. 20:1-18, including being the first to see Jesus alive from the dead, before joining the other women to go to the tomb just after sunrise.)

**Event 4.)** *[Time: Perhaps 4:15 a.m.]* **Distraught at the sight of the stone missing from the opening of the tomb, Mary Magdalene ran to report to Peter.**

Jn. 20:2 And so she ran and came to Simon Peter, and to the other disciple whom Jesus loved, and said to them, "They have taken away the Lord out of the tomb, and we do not know where they have laid Him."

**Event 5.)** *[Time: Perhaps 4:30 a.m.]* **Peter and the other disciple ran from their abode to the tomb, went inside, and saw the linen wrappings and face-cloth. The other disciple saw and believed that Jesus was alive from the dead; Peter saw the body was missing, but apparently, he did not believe Jesus was alive.**

Jn. 20:3 Peter therefore went forth, and the other disciple, and they were going to the tomb.
Jn. 20:4 And the two were running together; and the other disciple ran ahead faster than Peter, and came to the tomb first;
Jn. 20:5 and stooping and looking in, he saw the linen wrappings lying *there*; but he did not go in.
Jn. 20:6 Simon Peter therefore also came, following him, and entered the tomb; and he beheld the linen wrappings lying *there*,

Jn. 20:7 and the face-cloth, which had been on His head, not lying with the linen wrappings, but rolled up in a place by itself.

Jn. 20:8 So the other disciple who had first come to the tomb entered then also, and he saw and believed.

Jn. 20:9 For as yet they did not understand the Scripture, that He must rise again from the dead.

**Event 6.)** *[Time: Perhaps 4:40 a.m.]* **After telling Peter and the other disciple about the missing body, Mary Magdalene came along behind, returning to the tomb. Having inspected the tomb, the two men returned to their homes, leaving her alone. She bent down and looked inside and saw two angels sitting where the body of Jesus had been laid, one at the head and the other at the feet. They asked her why she was crying.**

Jn. 20:10 So the disciples went away again to their own homes.

Jn. 20:11 But Mary was standing outside the tomb weeping; and so, as she wept, she stooped and looked into the tomb;

Jn. 20:12 and she beheld two angels in white sitting, one at the head, and one at the feet, where the body of Jesus had been lying.

Jn. 20:13 And they said to her, "Woman, why are you weeping?" She said to them, "Because they have taken away my Lord, and I do not know where they have laid Him."

**Event 7.)** *[Time: 4:45 a.m.]* **Mary Magdalene then turned and looked out away from the tomb and saw someone standing nearby. He asked her why she was crying and who she was looking for. She assumed him to be the gardener and asked him where the body of Jesus might be. Jesus spoke her name, "Mary," and in an instant of joy and relief she recognized him and reached out to embrace him. He told her not to cling to him, explained why, and gave her a message to take to his brethren.**

Jn. 20:14 When she had said this, she turned around, and beheld Jesus standing *there*, and did not know that it was Jesus.

Jn. 20:15 Jesus said to her, "Woman, why are you weeping? Whom are you seeking?" Supposing Him to be the gardener, she said to Him, "Sir, if you have carried Him away, tell me where you have laid Him, and I will take Him away."

Jn. 20:16 Jesus said to her, "Mary!" She turned and said to Him in Hebrew, "Rabboni!" (which means, Teacher).

Jn. 20:17 Jesus said to her, "Stop clinging to Me, for I have not yet ascended to the Father; but go to My brethren, and say to them, 'I ascend to My Father and your Father, and My God and your God.' "

**Event 8.)** *[Time: About 5:00 a.m., Sunday morning]* **Having seen Jesus alive and having been given a message from Jesus to take to his brethren, Mary Magdalene returned to the abode of the male disciples and told them the great news that Jesus was alive, she had seen him with her own eyes, and he had given her a message to give to them. They did not believe her.**

Jn. 20:18 Mary Magdalene came, announcing to the disciples, "I have seen the Lord," and *that* He had said these things to her.

Mk. 16:9 Now after He had risen early on the first day of the week, He first appeared to Mary Magdalene, from whom He had cast out seven demons.

Mk. 16:10 She went and reported to those who had been with Him, while they were mourning and weeping.

Mk. 16:11 And when they heard that He was alive, and had been seen by her, they refused to believe it.

What we have seen thus far is a simple, straightforward weaving together of the accounts to form a new narrative, a more complete picture of everything that can be known about the particulars surrounding the resurrection of Christ. By distinguishing the pieces from the accounts and fitting them together in the manner set forth above, we know that Mary Magdalene and the other Mary went to look at the tomb on the evening of the Sabbath. Then, at some point in the early morning hours, the angel of the Lord descended from heaven, the soldiers passed out, and he rolled away the stone from the tomb to signify that God had raised Jesus from the dead. Soon afterwards, in the early morning hours of the first day of the week, Mary Magdalene ventured out alone to look again at the tomb. John 20:1 is plain about the timing of her trip: "on the first day of the week Mary Magdalene came early to the tomb, while it was still dark . . ." There can be no dispute about the merits of the 4:00 a.m. guess. It fits the description well. Given what had to be her state of shock and grief at Jesus' brutal death, Mary was likely having trouble sleeping. Looking at the grave of a lost loved-one is tough medicine, but often necessary. Since it can be calculated to be just past the middle of the month of Nisan, Mary was likely aided by the light of a nearly full, waning moon.

When Mary arrived at the tomb, she was the first to discover the stone missing. Alarmed, she ran to the acknowledged leader of the disciples, Peter. He and the unnamed disciple sprinted to the tomb, went inside and made an inspection, then emerged. By then, Mary had caught up with them and had returned to the site of the Lord's tomb. The unnamed disciple (Lazarus?) believed, while obviously Peter did not. The men returned to their homes (Lazarus had his own home in Bethany and would have gone to tell his sisters the good news) and left Mary Magdalene alone. It's reasonable that by now it could be around 4:45 am.

After bending down and seeing two angels in the tomb, Mary turned and saw someone near whom she assumed to be the gardener. Jesus called her name and Mary recognized him. He gave her a message to take to his brethren, which after being the first to see the Lord alive, she did. Imagine her joy. But what a blow it must have been for Mary when the men rejected her testimony and the message he entrusted to her. The cultural setting of the time didn't favor women getting involved in the business of men, and given the tension of the setting and the fact that she had already been there pounding on their door about an hour earlier, they likely dealt with her in a harsh manner. Mary then went to meet up with the other women and went with them to the tomb, arriving just after the sun had risen.

Chapter Five
# EPIPHANY IN AN EMPTY TOMB

**Event 9.)** *[Time: Shortly after sunrise 6:15 a.m., Sunday morning, Easter]* **The group of women (including Mary Magdalene) who followed Jesus from Galilee to Jerusalem, went together to the tomb of Jesus just after sunrise on the first day of the week. Their purpose was to gain access to the tomb if possible and to add their own spices to the body of Jesus. As they walked, they questioned who would roll away the stone for them. When they arrived at the tomb they found the stone already removed.**

Mk. 16:1 And when the Sabbath was over, Mary Magdalene, and Mary the *mother* of James, and Salome, bought spices, that they might come and anoint Him.

Mk. 16:2 And very early on the first day of the week, they came to the tomb when the sun had risen.

Mk. 16:3 And they were saying to one another, "Who will roll away the stone for us from the entrance of the tomb?"

Lk. 24:1 But on the first day of the week, at early dawn, they came to the tomb, bringing the spices which they had prepared.

Lk. 24:2 And they found the stone rolled away from the tomb,

(The group of women included Mary Magdalene (Mt. 28:1, Mk. 16:1, Lk. 24:10, Jn. 20:1), Mary the mother of James (Mt. 27:56, Lk. 24:10), Salome (Mk. 16:1), Johanna (Lk. 24:10), and others (Lk. 24:10). Around sunrise they traveled together to the tomb on Easter Sunday morning with the intent of gaining access and adding their purchased and prepared spices to the body of Jesus. It is interesting to note that as the women walked they talked about the problem of the stone which they expected to find over the entrance to the tomb (Mk. 16:3). Being careful students, we know that one woman in that group already knew the stone was not over the opening and that the body was missing. Evidently, Mary Magdalene wasn't telling what she knew. Let's put ourselves in her shoes and see if her silence may be understood as reasonable. If so, then we have the necessary means of transition to relate her predawn experiences to those that followed.

First, concerning consistency, all that must be acknowledged is the possibility that Mary Magdalene did not chime in on the "Who will roll away the stone for us?" discussion with the other women. But, why she didn't talk is a mystery worth looking into. Mary was a real person, and we need to consider how it felt to experience what she did on the morning of the resurrection. This may be why Mary is so prominently featured in the Easter narrative; because of her exceptional love for the Lord. Without cause to consider Mary's heart, the Easter story is just about people moving from one thing to another. She humanizes the events of that morning. For the Christian, Mary's devotion is an example worth noting.

Every Gospel mentions Mary Magdalene by name. Whenever a group of women are listed, her name appears first. Tracking her footsteps through Easter allows us to understand what happened and to tie it all together. First, let's review what we know.

By allowing the words of Scripture to hold true to their most obvious meaning, we learned that previous to her trip to the tomb with the women at sunrise (as told in Mark and Luke), Mary Magdalene ventured out to look upon the tomb "early... while it was still dark

(Jn. 20:1)." She was alarmed when she discovered the stone missing in the pre-dawn darkness of Easter morning. She ran to Peter, reported to him, and followed behind the men as they sprinted to the tomb. The men went inside to investigate, emerged, and left her alone. John's account then describes Mary's experience as the first person to see Jesus alive. The Lord gave her a message to take to his "brethren." Mark confirms John's chronology in 16:9-11 that Mary was the first to see Jesus alive from the dead and that she went and told the male disciples. In verse 11 Mark gives us an important detail that John didn't, that the men did NOT believe her. How do you think that felt?

Imagine Mary's roller coaster ride of emotions that morning. First, her panic upon discovering the stone missing. Then, her joy at discovering that Jesus was alive. She might well have felt lighter than air as she raced to tell the men the happy news and give them her message from the Lord. But when the men refused to believe, she must have been shocked and disappointed.

But from the men's perspective, consider how unstable Mary must have seemed. She had already knocked on their door around 4:00 a.m., distraught at having discovered the stone missing from the tomb. And then she was back again, bubbling over with joy and saying she had seen Jesus. Imagine how she must have seemed; picture her as spoke to the men, trying to catch her breath: "I turned and thought I was talking to the gardener, but it was the Lord. He called me by name. It was him. He's alive! I reached out to grab him and he told me not to cling to him. . .oh yes, and he gave me a message for you. He said, 'I ascend unto my God and your God and to my Father and your Father.' Isn't it wonderful?" By the end of her speech, Mary must have been looking into narrowed eyes--we know from Mark that she was not believed.

Remember that in eastern culture, then and in many places yet today, men ran the world. We also know that following the arrest of Jesus and his crucifixion, his core group of male disciples were hiding behind closed doors "for fear of the Jews (Jn. 20:19). How might they have felt about an excited woman running around telling others "Jesus is alive!?" It's also possible Peter, who may have been in an especially sour mood, could have rebuked her sharply.

And maybe Mary began to second guess herself. Culturally, it was quite preposterous that IF Jesus were somehow alive, that he would appear to a woman. Upon hearing her testimony, the male disciples may have mentioned this very fact to her. And it was dark ... and the whole "I ascend" thing is tough to understand, even for us today.

Another factor is Jesus specifically told Mary to tell "my brethren." Jesus did not require her to tell the women too. Her silence on the way to the tomb Easter morning could also simply be an act of obedience, Mary being certain that the Lord would reveal himself in his own way and at his own time.

And let me suggest one other possibility. There may have been some jealousy at work in the ranks. We know that there was among the male disciples at times. It takes little reading between the lines to know that Mary's love of Jesus was exceptional. Jesus was already breaking the rules of his day by allowing female disciples. These women were in a unique position. While we might assume they were a tight knit group, we don't know. If Mary told the other women of having seen Jesus, having been with him, alive from the dead (something none of the disciples were anticipating) what might Mary have feared them of accusing her of? Flights of fantasy? Delusion? Being in a fragile state, having had a morning packed with emotional extremes, and being sleep deprived, Mary may have felt that telling the other women may have had consequences she wasn't, at that time, prepared to deal with.

So, it seems Mary walked along with the other women to the tomb, biting her tongue as they discussed getting someone to remove the stone for them. It seems Mary was taking it all in, ready for whatever was going to happen next. After all, the specially chosen male disciples did not believe her story, so would she want to risk the same rejection by the women?

Whatever the case, the evidence suggests Mary wasn't telling what she knew. And considering how her experiences may have impacted her, it's not difficult to account for her silence. Just because we can't fully understand her actions, or what was going on in her heart, there's nothing about this small problem that rises to the level of contradiction.)

**Event 10.)** *[About a half hour after sunrise]* **The women entered the tomb, saw a total of three angels, one (the angel that had earlier rolled away the stone and sat on it) seated on the right side where the body of Jesus had lain, and then two more standing near them. The first angel gave them a message about the state of Jesus—"He has risen,"—and told them that they would see him in Galilee. The two angels reminded the women of what Jesus had told them, before his crucifixion, about his death and resurrection, which upon hearing they remembered his having told them.**

Mt. 28:5 And the angel answered and said to the women, "Do not be afraid; for I know that you are looking for Jesus who has been crucified.
Mt. 28:6 "He is not here, for He has risen, just as He said. Come, see the place where He was lying.
Mt. 28:7 "And go quickly and tell His disciples that He has risen from the dead; and behold, He is going before

you into Galilee, there you will see Him; behold, I have told you."

Mk. 16:4 And looking up, they saw that the stone had been rolled away, although it was extremely large.

Mk. 16:5 And entering the tomb, they saw a young man sitting at the right, wearing a white robe; and they were amazed.

Mk. 16:6 And he said to them, "Do not be amazed; you are looking for Jesus the Nazarene, who has been crucified. He has risen; He is not here; behold, *here* is the place where they laid Him.

Mk. 16:7 "But go, tell His disciples and Peter, 'He is going before you into Galilee; there you will see Him, just as He said to you.'"

Lk. 24:3 but when they entered, they did not find the body of the Lord Jesus.

Lk. 24:4 And it happened that while they were perplexed about this, behold, two men suddenly stood near them in dazzling apparel;

Lk. 24:5 and as *the women* were terrified and bowed their faces to the ground, *the men* said to them, "Why do you seek the living One among the dead?

Lk. 24:6 "He is not here, but He has risen. Remember how He spoke to you while He was still in Galilee,

Lk. 24:7 saying that the Son of Man must be delivered into the hands of sinful men, and be crucified, and the third day rise again."

Lk. 24:8 And they remembered His words,

(Determining the number of angels in the tomb on Easter morning is a matter of simple addition. Let's do the math.

First, it is not a problem that the writers interchangeably referred to the same beings as young men or angels. We may well conclude that the angels had the appearance of young men, consistent with what would be expected of trusted faithful messengers.

Concerning the seated young man [angel] on the right side in Mark, he is clearly the same angel of Matthew that earlier [between midnight and 3:00 — Event 2] rolled the stone away and sat on it. This fact is established by his speech to the women which is virtually the same in Matthew and Mark. Matthew says he appeared and rolled the stone away, but doesn't say when. Then he writes of him speaking to the women, but doesn't say when or where; we learn that from Mark.

Though complex, Matthew 28 is easily resolved by acknowledging the existence of a gap of time of several hours between vss. 1 and 2 [between the trip of the two Marys "to see" the tomb Sabbath evening and the angel's dramatic appearance to roll away the stone] and another gap between vss. 4 and 5 [between the angel's sitting upon the stone and his speaking to the women after sunrise in the tomb seated on the right side].

Luke is clearly writing of the identical event as Mark [the women going to spice the body and entering the tomb after arriving just after sunrise on Easter morning] and reveals they saw two angels that appeared standing next to them. The seated angel of Mark [identical with Matthew's] told the women that Jesus had been raised from the dead and they were to go to Galilee. The speech of the two standing angels served to remind the women that Jesus had, before his crucifixion, foretold his resurrection; something the women then remembered.

The seated angel of Mark and the two standing angels of Luke are not contradictory depictions of the same angel, but clearly different descriptions of different angels, in different positions, and giving the women different speeches. Adding the accounts together, the conclusion is warranted: in the tomb on Easter morning the faithful women saw a total of three angels.)

**Event 11.)** *[Perhaps 40 minutes after sunrise]* **Having seen the angels, the women, scared speechless, ran from the tomb. Jesus appeared to them. They held him by the feet and worshipped him. The Lord confirmed what they had just heard from the angels, that they would see him in Galilee. He told the women to tell the men to get going, that they would see him there.**

Mt. 28:8 And they departed quickly from the tomb with fear and great joy and ran to report it to His disciples.
Mt. 28:9 And behold, Jesus met them and greeted them. And they came up and took hold of His feet and worshiped Him.
Mt. 28:10 Then Jesus said to them, "Do not be afraid; go and take word to My brethren to leave for Galilee, and there they shall see Me."
Mk. 16:8 And they went out and fled from the tomb, for trembling and astonishment had gripped them; and they said nothing to anyone, for they were afraid.

(The records are accused of contradiction here in that in Mark it says, "they fled from the tomb ... and said nothing to anyone," while in Luke 24:9 it says they "returned from the tomb and reported all these things to the eleven and to all the rest." Mark clearly says why they didn't speak, "for they were afraid." Critics are fond of accusing the accounts of contradiction on this point; but to prove it they would have to argue that the women never recovered from their immediate fear or ever spoke of their encounter with the angels in the tomb.

Mark's obvious point is that they were so frightened as they fled they didn't stop to talk about it amongst themselves. Today we would say, "they were scared speechless." Adding the pieces of information together, it's obvious what happened and that the accounts agree. Being frightened, without having to talk to one another about what to do, they all ran to tell the disciples, an obvious choice. As they ran, Jesus appeared to them and began his speech with the comforting words "Fear not." The women fell at his feet and worshipped him. Seeing Jesus, being with him, relieved their initial fears (if not their excitement) and the women then continued from there to testify to the men. No problem and no contradiction.

In some Bible versions contradiction is also commonly alleged here concerning the fact that the women were allowed to touch Jesus, they "took hold of his feet;" while in John, when Jesus first appeared to Mary Magdalene in early morning darkness, He forbade her to touch Him, explaining, "for I am not yet ascended unto the Father (John 20:17)." A possible accounting for this can be found by noting that these two events are separated by at least an hour or more. Though we can't know exactly what it was Jesus needed to yet fulfill by ascending to His Father when He first appeared to Mary Magdalene, it is reasonable to allow that He fulfilled this requirement in this interim period between His appearance to her and His appearance to the group of frightened women who fled the tomb after sunrise. Even less troublesome is the fact that some Bible versions translate his prohibition as "don't cling to me." This is the way our NASB provides the phrase and is likely the most accurate. From this sense it may be understood that in saying, "don't cling to me" Jesus was telling Mary that things had changed and he was going to be ascending to his Father. The time for clinging to him (either physically or in a dependent sense) had passed.

Jesus did not spend a lot of time with his disciples during the forty days between his resurrection and ascension. Why not? It seems reasonable that his purpose was to give his disciples sufficient evidence that he had risen from death, but not to spend so much time with them would that they would count upon him being around, at least in physical form. His several appearances, spaced out over the forty days, were evidential and instructional with a view to preparing them to receive and depend upon the Holy Spirit.)

**Event 12.)** *[About an hour after sunrise]* **Having seen Jesus and been comforted by him, the women went to tell the disciples about their experience. As they were going, the soldiers who had passed out at the sight of the angel earlier that morning started to make their way into the city. Rather than report their failure to secure the tomb to their Roman military superiors, they went to the chief priests and received money to lie about what had happened. The soldiers were also given assurance by the religious leaders that if it became necessary they would intervene with Pilate to keep them out of trouble.**

Mt. 28:11 Now while they were on their way, behold, some of the guard came into the city and reported to the chief priests all that had happened.
Mt. 28:12 And when they had assembled with the elders and counseled together, they gave a large sum of money to the soldiers,
Mt. 28:13 and said, "You are to say, 'His disciples came by night and stole Him away while we were asleep.'
Mt. 28:14 "And if this should come to the governor's ears, we will win him over and keep you out of trouble."
Mt. 28:15 And they took the money and did as they had been instructed; and this story was widely spread among the Jews, *and is* to this day.

**Event 13.)** *[Time: About an hour after sunrise]* **Having experienced the angels in the tomb and having seen Jesus, the group of women (including Mary M, her second report to the men of having seen Jesus alive) went and told the male disciples what they had experienced and the message from Jesus to head to back to Galilee, that they would see him there. The men did not believe the women.**

> Lk. 24:9 and returned from the tomb and reported all these things to the eleven and to all the rest.
> Lk. 24:10 Now they were Mary Magdalene and Joanna and Mary the *mother* of James; also the other women with them were telling these things to the apostles.
> Lk. 24:11 And these words appeared to them as nonsense, and they would not believe them.

**Event 14.)** *[Time: Perhaps 7:00 a.m.]* **Upon hearing what the women reported, Peter ran to the tomb for the second time.**

> Lk. 24:12 But Peter arose and ran to the tomb; stooping and looking in, he saw the linen wrappings only; and he went away to his home, marveling at that which had happened.

## SUMMARY

The women met and walked together to the tomb, arriving just after sunrise on what we call Easter Sunday. When they arrived the women found the stone missing from the tomb and went inside. According to Mark they found a young man seated on the right side where the body of Jesus had laid. There is outstanding complexity here, but it all fits together. The first thing to observe is that the speech of this angel in Mark is identical to that of the angel in Matthew, identifying them as one and the same. Matthew's account may be seen as true and completed by the extra details provided by Mark. The angel who rolled away the stone and sat on it to signify the resurrection of Jesus was, by the time the women entered the tomb, seated inside the tomb on the right side. Matthew says the angel spoke to the women (Mary M. and the other Mary in 28:1) and Mark confirms in 16:1 that both these women (and others with them) were included in the group that entered the tomb and encountered the angel.

Additionally, from Luke we learn that two other angels appeared to the women, standing near them. While the seated angel on the right announced the resurrection and that they were to return to Galilee, the two angels standing near the women reminded them that Jesus had foretold his resurrection before he was crucified.

The women ran from the tomb, too frightened to stop and talk amongst themselves about their experience. They made a beeline to go tell the men and as they ran, Jesus appeared to them. They fell before him, held him by the feet in worship, and he confirmed what the angels had just told them about returning to Galilee.

When the mighty angel of the Lord appeared at the sight of the tomb amid a shaking earth and wearing lightening-like garments the Roman soldiers who had been guarding the tomb, had passed out. After coming to, they must have hidden themselves. As the women went to tell the disciples of their experience, the soldiers returned to the city. But rather than report to their superiors, they went to the priests and received bribe money to lie about what had happened.

Having seen Jesus and overcoming their initial sudden fear at having seen the angels in the tomb, the women told their story to the eleven and all the rest and were not believed. But Peter ran to the tomb to inspect for the second time that morning. Though similar to John's record, allowing the Scripture to say what it means this sprint by Peter must be seen as different. The details reveal three distinctions to be made.

1.) *The time of day*: Peter's first sprint in John 20 happened before Jesus appeared to Mary Magdalene. Remember she was out "early, when it was yet dark (John 20:1)." In contrast, it is plain that Peter's run to tomb described in Luke 24:12 happened well *after* sunrise.

2.) _The stimulus that prompted him_: His first sprint was the result of Magdalene's alarming report "they have taken away the Lord out of the sepulcher (John 20:2)." But this second run to the tomb was prompted by the joyous report of the group of women who saw the angels in the sepulcher; had seen Jesus with their own eyes; and had held him by the feet (Matthew).

3.) _The result_: In John 20 it may be safely inferred that after seeing the burial clothes during his venture into the tomb (in the pre-dawn darkness), Peter did not believe that Jesus had been resurrected. Contrast that however with the result following his second trip to the tomb: He "departed, wondering in himself at that which was come to pass (Luke 24:12)." This doesn't mean he believed but it shows that he was warming up to the idea that something fantastic had happened.

According to Paul's list of the resurrection appearances of Jesus, the Lord appeared to Peter some time after he left the tomb. For the sake of simplicity we'll save Paul's list in 1 Cor. 15:3-8. After we've harmonized the Gospels and Acts, we'll integrate the six appearances of Jesus listed by Paul into the others.

# Chapter Six

# OPENING SCRIPTURES AND EYES

**Event 15.)** *[Perhaps 9:00 a.m., Sunday morning]* **Jesus appeared to two men, one of whom was named Cleopas, as they walked from Jerusalem toward Emmaus. Jesus joined with them and told them many things about himself from the scriptures of the Old Testament. He kept his identity hidden during this walk. Later he vanished when they recognized him as he gave thanks for their meal.** *[About 2:00 p.m.].*

Mk. 16:12 And after that, He appeared in a different form to two of them, while they were walking along on their way to the country.

Lk. 24:13 And behold, two of them were going that very day to a village named Emmaus, which was about seven miles from Jerusalem.
Lk. 24:14 And they were conversing with each other about all these things which had taken place.
Lk. 24:15 And it came about that while they were conversing and discussing, Jesus Himself approached, and *began* traveling with them.
Lk. 24:16 But their eyes were prevented from recognizing Him.
Lk. 24:17 And He said to them, "What are these words that you are exchanging with one another as you are walking?" And they stood still, looking sad.
Lk. 24:18 And one of them, named Cleopas, answered and said to Him, "Are You the only one visiting Jerusalem and unaware of the things which have happened here in these days?"
Lk. 24:19 And He said to them, "What things?" And they said to Him, "The things about Jesus the Nazarene, who

was a prophet mighty in deed and word in the sight of God and all the people,

Lk. 24:20 and how the chief priests and our rulers delivered Him up to the sentence of death, and crucified Him.

Lk. 24:21 "But we were hoping that it was He who was going to redeem Israel. Indeed, besides all this, it is the third day since these things happened.

Lk. 24:22 "But also some women among us amazed us. When they were at the tomb early in the morning,

Lk. 24:23 and did not find His body, they came, saying that they had also seen a vision of angels, who said that He was alive.

Lk. 24:24 "And some of those who were with us went to the tomb and found it just exactly as the women also had said; but Him they did not see."

Lk. 24:25 And He said to them, "O foolish men and slow of heart to believe in all that the prophets have spoken!

Lk. 24:26 "Was it not necessary for the Christ to suffer these things and to enter into His glory?"

Lk. 24:27 And beginning with Moses and with all the prophets, He explained to them the things concerning Himself in all the Scriptures.

Lk. 24:28 And they approached the village where they were going, and He acted as though He would go farther.

Lk. 24:29 And they urged Him, saying, "Stay with us, for it is *getting* toward evening, and the day is now nearly over." And He went in to stay with them.

Lk. 24:30 And it came about that when He had reclined *at the table* with them, He took the bread and blessed *it*, and breaking *it*, He *began* giving *it* to them.

Lk. 24:31 And their eyes were opened and they recognized Him; and He vanished from their sight.

Lk. 24:32 And they said to one another, "Were not our hearts burning within us while He was speaking to us on the road, while He was explaining the Scriptures to us?"

(It's been suggest that perhaps the other disciple with Cleopas might have been the apostle Peter. That doesn't really fit because in Lk. 24:33 it says these two returned to Jerusalem and found "the eleven" gathered together there. You could then argue that "the eleven" didn't really mean "*the* eleven," but why strain at such things when nothing is gained?)

**Event 16.)** *[About 5:00 p.m., Sunday]* **These two men then returned to Jerusalem to tell the others of having been with Jesus. They walked in on a discussion taking place among the eleven and the other disciples gathered concerning the appearance of Jesus to Peter. The two from the road to Emmaus told their story to the disciples and were not believed.**

Mk. 16:13 And they went away and reported it to the others, but they did not believe them either.

Lk. 24:33 And they arose that very hour and returned to Jerusalem, and found gathered together the eleven and those who were with them,
Lk. 24:34 saying, "The Lord has really risen, and has appeared to Simon."
Lk. 24:35 And they *began* to relate their experiences on the road and how He was recognized by them in the breaking of the bread.

(There is a contradiction indicated in the foregoing, but it's not an error in the text, but a contradiction that is common to human nature. Peter testified of having seen the Lord alive from the dead, but the disciples that were gathered together did not really believe him. From what can be known of Peter's impetuous and confrontational personality from other records in the scripture, it's understandable why the disciples

61

would act like they believed his testimony, while in their hearts they did not.)

**Event 17.)** *[About 5:15 p.m., Sunday evening]* **As the two witnesses from the Emmaus Road were rehearsing their experiences, Jesus himself appeared in the midst of the closed room. The disciple Thomas had been there when the two Emmaus Road witnesses had arrived, but he left while the two were telling their story, before Jesus appeared.**

Lk. 24:36 And while they were telling these things, He Himself stood in their midst.

Lk. 24:37 But they were startled and frightened and thought that they were seeing a spirit.

Lk. 24:38 And He said to them, "Why are you troubled, and why do doubts arise in your hearts?

Lk. 24:39 "See My hands and My feet, that it is I Myself; touch Me and see, for a spirit does not have flesh and bones as you see that I have."

Lk. 24:40 And when He had said this, He showed them His hands and His feet.

Lk. 24:41 And while they still could not believe it for joy and were marveling, He said to them, "Have you anything here to eat?"

Lk. 24:42 And they gave Him a piece of a broiled fish;

Lk. 24:43 and He took it and ate it before them.

Lk. 24:44 Now He said to them, "These are My words which I spoke to you while I was still with you, that all things which are written about Me in the Law of Moses and the Prophets and the Psalms must be fulfilled."

Lk. 24:45 Then He opened their minds to understand the Scriptures,

Lk. 24:46 and He said to them, "Thus it is written, that the Christ should suffer and rise again from the dead the third day;

Lk. 24:47 and that repentance for forgiveness of sins should be proclaimed in His name to all the nations, beginning from Jerusalem.

Lk. 24:48 "You are witnesses of these things.

Lk. 24:49 "And behold, I am sending forth the promise of My Father upon you; but you are to stay in the city until you are clothed with power from on high."


Jn. 20:19 When therefore it was evening, on that day, the first *day* of the week, and when the doors were shut where the disciples were, for fear of the Jews, Jesus came and stood in their midst, and said to them, "Peace *be* with you."

Jn. 20:20 And when He had said this, He showed them both His hands and His side. The disciples therefore rejoiced when they saw the Lord.

Jn. 20:21 Jesus therefore said to them again, "Peace *be* with you; as the Father has sent Me, I also send you."

Jn. 20:22 And when He had said this, He breathed on them, and said to them, "Receive the Holy Spirit.

Jn. 20:23 "If you forgive the sins of any, *their sins* have been forgiven them; if you retain the *sins* of any, they have been retained."

Jn. 20:24 But Thomas, one of the twelve, called Didymus, was not with them when Jesus came.

Jn. 20:25 The other disciples therefore were saying to him, "We have seen the Lord!" But he said to them, "Unless I shall see in His hands the imprint of the nails, and put my finger into the place of the nails, and put my hand into His side, I will not believe."

## SUMMARY

Having been at the tomb, seeing the angels, and encountering Jesus as they fled, the group of women went to the home of the male disciples and told their story (Lk. 24:9). Their story was not believed. Among that group of men were two (Luke reveals one of their names as Cleopas) who soon afterward began walking toward Emmaus. As they walked along, a stranger joined himself to them. He directed the conversation towards the source of their sadness, the death of Jesus, and then began a lengthy discourse about the Old Testament promises of the Messiah and his mission. At the end of their journey they persuaded the stranger to join them in a meal and as he blessed it, they recognized Jesus and he vanished from their sight. Afterward they commented, "Were not our hearts burning within us while He was speaking to us on the road…" As the stranger opened the Scriptures they were thrilled to see that the narrative of the life of Jesus matched the Old Testament promises and prophecies of the Messiah.

The two men rushed back to Jerusalem and found the disciples gathered. When they walked in they were told "the Lord is risen indeed and has appeared to Peter." Although they gave their voices in assenting to Peter's testimony, the roomful of disciples apparently did not believe. They doubted the truth behind the Emmaus witnesses' testimony as well.

We know from Lk. 24:33 that when the Emmaus witness arrived they "found gathered together the eleven and those who were with them," but while they were sharing their story, it seems that Thomas must have left the room. He'd heard numerous reports all day long of the resurrection of Jesus, and perhaps he couldn't bear to hear any more.

As the two men were telling their extended story of having been with the stranger who opened the Scriptures, Jesus appeared in the midst of the closed room. He offered them proof that it was really him, that he was alive in the same wounded body he had died in, and ate food in their sight. He began to prepare them for their future ministries and to direct them in the receiving of the Holy Spirit.

# Chapter Seven

# TO THE TOP OF THE MOUNTAIN AND BACK

A CAREFUL STUDY documents eleven distinct resurrection appearances of Jesus before his ascension. Of these, five were to the male disciples as a larger group. These group appearances seem to be spaced out somewhat evenly over the forty-day period. We've covered the first group appearance in the last chapter. Now we'll look at the last four, including the final appearance of Jesus on the occasion of the ascension.

**Event 18.)** *[Time: Eight days after the resurrection]* **Eight Days later, Jesus appeared to the group of the disciples for the second time. Jesus continued preparing them for future ministry and singled out Thomas, addressing his concerns and confronting his unbelief.**

> Mk. 16:14 And afterward He appeared to the eleven themselves as they were reclining *at the table*; and He reproached them for their unbelief and hardness of heart, because they had not believed those who had seen Him after He had risen.
>
> Mk. 16:15 And He said to them, "Go into all the world and preach the gospel to all creation.
>
> Mk. 16:16 "He who has believed and has been baptized shall be saved; but he who has disbelieved shall be condemned.
>
> Mk. 16:17 "And these signs will accompany those who have believed: in My name they will cast out demons, they will speak with new tongues;
>
> Mk. 16:18 they will pick up serpents, and if they drink any deadly *poison*, it shall not hurt them; they will lay hands on the sick, and they will recover."

Jn. 20:26 And after eight days again His disciples were inside, and Thomas with them. Jesus came, the doors having been shut, and stood in their midst, and said, "Peace *be* with you."

Jn. 20:27 Then He said to Thomas, "Reach here your finger, and see My hands; and reach here your hand, and put it into My side; and be not unbelieving, but believing."

Jn. 20:28 Thomas answered and said to Him, "My Lord and my God!"

Jn. 20:29 Jesus said to him, "Because you have seen Me, have you believed? Blessed *are* they who did not see, and yet believed."

Jn. 20:30 Many other signs therefore Jesus also performed in the presence of the disciples, which are not written in this book;

Jn. 20:31 but these have been written that you may believe that Jesus is the Christ, the Son of God; and that believing you may have life in His name.

(If the term "the eleven" in Mark was granted to be a kind of general appellation attached to the remaining core group [following the death of Judas] of Jesus' disciples, then it might be possible to designate the resurrection appearance of Jesus described in Mark as being identical with his first on the afternoon of Easter. But this is not something that critics will likely grant. So then, in interest of simplicity and remembering the goal of putting the accounts together "without contradiction," I chose to join Mark's resurrection appearance of Jesus as identical with his second in Jn. 20:26. In the second group appearance described in John all of "the eleven" were present, Thomas being singled out. In the group appearance described by Mark, he identifies that it was to "the eleven." In simplest terms, that includes Thomas. From this criteria Mk. 16:14-18 meshes together with Jn. 20:26-31 in suitable fashion and leaves the critic with no rationale by which to continue to insist the accounts are contradictory. In the group appearance described by Mark it is important to note that he does not say Jesus appeared *only* to the eleven on this occasion. It's likely other disciples were present as well. This will be important later. It's reasonable that by this time (eight days later per John) they were on their way back to Galilee with all the disciples who had gone to Jerusalem with them.

It's worth mentioning that the writer of Mark jumped from his accounting of the group of women telling their story to the disciples in verse 13 to the appearance of Jesus in verse 14. The writer did so with nothing more than the words, "and afterward." This connective does not mean "immediately afterward," but is just another example of the tendency of the Gospel writers to jump from one event to a distant other without specifying the passing of time in between.)

**Event 19.)** *[Time: In the morning, perhaps two weeks after the resurrection of Jesus]* **Jesus appeared again to a group of the disciples, this time on the shore of the Sea of Galilee (also called Tiberius). This was his third recorded appearance to a group of the disciples.**

Jn. 21:1 After these things Jesus manifested Himself again to the disciples at the Sea of Tiberias, and He manifested *Himself* in this way.
Jn. 21:2 There were together Simon Peter, and Thomas called Didymus, and Nathanael of Cana in Galilee, and the *sons* of Zebedee, and two others of His disciples.
Jn. 21:3 Simon Peter said to them, "I am going fishing." They said to him, "We will also come with you." They went out, and got into the boat; and that night they caught nothing.

Jn. 21:4 But when the day was now breaking, Jesus stood on the beach; yet the disciples did not know that it was Jesus.

Jn. 21:5 Jesus therefore said to them, "Children, you do not have any fish, do you?" They answered Him, "No."

Jn. 21:6 And He said to them, "Cast the net on the right-hand side of the boat, and you will find a catch." They cast therefore, and then they were not able to haul it in because of the great number of fish.

Jn. 21:7 That disciple therefore whom Jesus loved said to Peter, "It is the Lord." And so when Simon Peter heard that it was the Lord, he put his outer garment on (for he was stripped *for work*), and threw himself into the sea.

Jn. 21:8 But the other disciples came in the little boat, for they were not far from the land, but about one hundred yards away, dragging the net *full* of fish.

Jn. 21:9 And so when they got out upon the land, they saw a charcoal fire *already* laid, and fish placed on it, and bread.

Jn. 21:10 Jesus said to them, "Bring some of the fish which you have now caught."

Jn. 21:11 Simon Peter went up, and drew the net to land, full of large fish, a hundred and fifty-three; and although there were so many, the net was not torn.

Jn. 21:12 Jesus said to them, "Come *and* have breakfast." None of the disciples ventured to question Him, "Who are You?" knowing that it was the Lord.

Jn. 21:13 Jesus came and took the bread, and gave them, and the fish likewise.

Jn. 21:14 This is now the third time that Jesus was manifested to the disciples, after He was raised from the dead.

Jn. 21:15 So when they had finished breakfast, Jesus said to Simon Peter, "Simon, *son* of John, do you love Me more than these?" He said to Him, "Yes, Lord; You know that I love You." He said to him, "Tend My lambs."

Jn. 21:16 He said to him again a second time, "Simon, *son* of John, do you love Me?" He said to Him, "Yes, Lord; You know that I love You." He said to him, "Shepherd My sheep."

Jn. 21:17 He said to him the third time, "Simon, *son* of John, do you love Me?" Peter was grieved because He said to him the third time, "Do you love Me?" And he said to Him, "Lord, You know all things; You know that I love You." Jesus said to him, "Tend My sheep.

Jn. 21:18 "Truly, truly, I say to you, when you were younger, you used to gird yourself, and walk wherever you wished; but when you grow old, you will stretch out your hands, and someone else will gird you, and bring you where you do not wish to go."

Jn. 21:19 Now this He said, signifying by what kind of death he would glorify God. And when He had spoken this, He said to him, "Follow Me!"

Jn. 21:20 Peter, turning around, saw the disciple whom Jesus loved following *them*; the one who also had leaned back on His breast at the supper, and said, "Lord, who is the one who betrays You?"

Jn. 21:21 Peter therefore seeing him said to Jesus, "Lord, and what about this man?"

Jn. 21:22 Jesus said to him, "If I want him to remain until I come, what is *that* to you? You follow Me!"

Jn. 21:23 This saying therefore went out among the brethren that that disciple would not die; yet Jesus did not say to him that he would not die, but *only*, "If I want him to remain until I come, what is that to you?"

Jn. 21:24 This is the disciple who bears witness of these things, and wrote these things; and we know that his witness is true.

Jn. 21:25 And there are also many other things which Jesus did, which if they were written in detail, I suppose that even the world itself would not contain the books which were written.

**Event 20.)** *[Time: Perhaps three weeks after the resurrection]* **Having obeyed Jesus and returned to Galilee, the fourth appearance of Jesus to the disciples was to only the eleven on a mountain that he had chosen.**

> Mt. 28:16 But the eleven disciples proceeded to Galilee, to the mountain which Jesus had designated.
> Mt. 28:17 And when they saw *Him*, they worshiped Him; but some were doubtful.
> Mt. 28:18 And Jesus came up and spoke to them, saying, "All authority has been given to Me in heaven and on earth.
> Mt. 28:19 "Go therefore and make disciples of all the nations, baptizing them in the name of the Father and the Son and the Holy Spirit,
> Mt. 28:20 teaching them to observe all that I commanded you; and lo, I am with you always, even to the end of the age."

**Event 21.)** *[Time: Forty days after the resurrection]* **The fifth — and last — resurrection appearance of Jesus to the disciples was on the occasion of his ascension into heaven.**

> Mk. 16:19 So then, when the Lord Jesus had spoken to them, He was received up into heaven, and sat down at the right hand of God.
> Mk. 16:20 And they went out and preached everywhere, while the Lord worked with them, and confirmed the word by the signs that followed.

> Lk. 24:50 And He led them out as far as Bethany, and He lifted up His hands and blessed them.
> Lk. 24:51 And it came about that while He was blessing them, He parted from them.
> Lk. 24:52 And they returned to Jerusalem with great joy,
> Lk. 24:53 and were continually in the temple, praising God.

Act 1:1 The first account I composed, Theophilus, about all that Jesus began to do and teach,

Act 1:2 until the day when He was taken up, after He had by the Holy Spirit given orders to the apostles whom He had chosen.

Act 1:3 To these He also presented Himself alive, after His suffering, by many convincing proofs, appearing to them over *a period of forty days*, and speaking of the things concerning the kingdom of God.

Act 1:4 And gathering them together, He commanded them not to leave Jerusalem, but to wait for what the Father had promised, *"Which," He said*, "you heard of from Me;

Act 1:5 for John baptized with water, but you shall be baptized with the Holy Spirit not many days from now."

Act 1:6 And so when they had come together, they were asking Him, saying, "Lord, is it at this time You are restoring the kingdom to Israel?"

Act 1:7 He said to them, "It is not for you to know times or epochs which the Father has fixed by His own authority;

Act 1:8 but you shall receive power when the Holy Spirit has come upon you; and you shall be My witnesses both in Jerusalem, and in all Judea and Samaria, and even to the remotest part of the earth."

Act 1:9 And after He had said these things, He was lifted up while they were looking on, and a cloud received Him out of their sight.

Act 1:10 And as they were gazing intently into the sky while He was departing, behold, two men in white clothing stood beside them;

Act 1:11 and they also said, "Men of Galilee, why do you stand looking into the sky? This Jesus, who has been taken up from you into heaven, will come in just the same way as you have watched Him go into heaven."

Act 1:12 Then they returned to Jerusalem from the mount called Olivet, which is near Jerusalem, a Sabbath day's journey away.

# SUMMARY

Even before his crucifixion, Jesus had instructed the disciples that he would go before them into Galilee (Mt. 26:32). But along with his statement about being raised, they neglected to hear his words. Following his resurrection, he sent word to the men by the women to return to Galilee. They did not pack up and head out, but disbelieved. Finally, after they saw Jesus for themselves they obeyed. Both John and Matthew confirm that they returned to the Galilee region. It seems evident that the appearance of Jesus on the appointed mountain must have been especially significant. On this appointed mountain overlooking their homeland where they had traveled and ministered with Jesus, the resurrected Lord of glory stood before his eleven chosen disciples. Certainly more was done and said on this important occasion than recorded in Matthew, but we do know the Lord spoke of the authority that had been given to him and commissioned these men to go into the nations of the world and make disciples in his name.

The disciples then returned to Jerusalem where the Lord appeared to them as a group for the fifth and final time. He led them out to Bethany, which was built up against the Mount of Olives, and ascended as they watched.

Chapter Eight
# THE APOSTLE PAUL'S SIX BULLETS

THE LAST REMAINING THING to do in reconciling the resurrection accounts is to integrate the six appearances of Christ listed in bullet point fashion by the apostle Paul in 1 Corinthians 15 into those already put into chronological order.

Critics are fond of faulting Paul for listing *only six* resurrection appearances of Jesus. I would think that six would be enough to prove his point (Jesus was resurrected and seen of many witnesses). But being eager to fault the accounts on every conceivable point, opponents reason that because Paul did not list the appearance of Jesus to Mary Magdalene (for example) that his omission amounts to an error on his part. They want to spin this to be as errant as if Paul had written "And that he was 'first' seen of Cephas." But Paul did not use the word "first," he only listed Jesus' appearance to Peter first. The exclusion of the appearance to Mary Magdalene (and others) does not prove Paul did not know of the others or that his list is contradictory because of its incompleteness. Just because a writer only tells a part of a story does not prove the part he gives is false.

Paul's exclusion of the women in his list is likely due to the cultural beliefs, which were predisposed to be biased against women's testimony. It's certainly fair to say his list is incomplete, but contradiction should not be granted unless it can be proved.

Paul's list in 1 Corinthians 15 is important for another reason. The first five appearances listed by the apostle were likely a part of an early creed, which became a part of Christianity within a few years after Jesus departed. According to Dr. Gary Habermas who has conducted extensive research on the opinions of modern authorities concerning the resurrection accounts, "most scholars who address the issue think that this testimony predates any New Testament book[7]." This evidence argues against the theory that the resurrection is a myth which grew with the telling and retelling in the early Christian communities.

Here then is Paul's list from 1 Corinthians.

(1 Co. 15:3) For I delivered unto you first of all that which I also received, how that Christ died for our sins according to the scriptures;

(1 Co. 15:4) And that he was buried, and that he rose again the third day according to the scriptures:

(1 Co. 15:5) And that he was seen of Cephas, then of the twelve:

(1 Co. 15:6) After that, he was seen of above five hundred brethren at once; of whom the greater part remain unto this present, but some are fallen asleep.

(1 Co. 15:7) After that, he was seen of James; then of all the apostles.

(1 Co. 15:8) And last of all he was seen of me also, as of one born out of due time.

For the sake of simplicity, these six appearances listed by Paul are listed below as A through F:

A. Seen by Cephas (Simon Peter)
B. Then by the Twelve
C. Seen by more than 500 brethren at once
D. Seen by James (the Lord's brother)
E. Then by all the apostles
F. Lastly by the apostle Paul

Now that these six provided in Paul's list have been labeled A through F, they may be integrated below in a master list of all the resurrection appearances of Jesus as chronicled in our previous study of the four gospels and Acts.

1. First, to Mary Magdalene alone in the garden in the pre-dawn darkness. (Event 7)

2. To the group of women after having seen and heard from the angels in the tomb. As they fled the tomb, they encountered Jesus, held him by the feet, and worshipped him. This was shortly after sunrise on the first day of the week. (Event 11)

3. (A.) To Peter, sometime after having visited the tomb for the second time, "wondering in himself at that which was come to pass," and before the two disciples arrived from the road to Emmaus. (See event 16)

4. To Cleopas and the other disciple (not named) on the road to Emmaus. These two returned to the eleven to find them talking excitedly about Jesus' appearance to Peter. (Event 15)

5. To the disciples behind closed doors, while the Emmaus witnesses were recounting their walk with the Lord, shortly after "doubting Thomas" left. (Event 17)

6. (B.) Eight days later as they sat at meat, Jesus appeared to the disciples ("the twelve" of 1 Corinthians 15:5) including Thomas, and to Matthias, who would later be numbered as the twelfth apostle, replacing Judas who had betrayed the Lord and committed suicide. As stated in Acts 1:15-26, a disciple named Matthias was voted in and numbered with the apostles, restoring the original number and group of "the twelve." The choice and inclusion of Matthias was made after the ascension of Christ and before the Day of Pentecost; and that this restored group was called "the twelve" after Matthias was added is confirmed in Acts 6:2. It is not then a problem that when Paul wrote his first letter to the church at Corinth (some twenty years after Matthias was added) that he would refer to them as "the twelve," even though at the time Jesus appeared to them Matthias had not yet been voted

in. It is credible to identify the second group appearance of Jesus (Event 18) as the one which would have included Matthias because Thomas would have had to have been present as well (which he wasn't at the first). Nothing is stated in either Mark or John that excludes the possibility that Matthias and/or other disciples were also present when Jesus appeared as they sat at a table (probably eating), eight days after his first appearance.

7. (C.) To more than 500 brethren at once, the majority of who were still alive at the time Paul penned his first letter to the church at Corinth.

8. (D.) To James the Lord's brother, who was given the office of an apostle and became the head pastor of the Christian church in Jerusalem.

9. To the disciples as a small group for the third time on the seashore. (Event 19)

10. (E.) To "the eleven" (as opposed to "the twelve," implying that no other disciples, not even Matthias, were present on this special occasion) on an appointed mountain in Galilee, which was the fourth known appearance to a group of disciples. (Event 20)

11. To "all the apostles," at the ascension, including Matthias and James the Lord's brother, near Bethany on the Mount of Olives. (Event 21)

12. (F.) To the apostle Paul "as one born out of due time."

Chapter Nine
# CONCLUSION

WITH THE QUEST for consistency as guide, the goal of fitting the pieces together in one narrative without contradiction seems to have been accomplished. The natural constraints of sense and logic are the glue which holds it together. If this is granted, it may be said that God gave his greatest story to the world as a type of literary puzzle, one that easily refutes any accusation of collusion, creates interdependence among the accounts, and when reconciled, gives the accounts an infusion of reliability.

If indeed the only requirement imposed by the Easter Challenge is to assemble all the verses relative to the resurrection of Jesus and his appearances together into one consistent narrative without contradiction, then it appears the Challenge has been answered successfully. I realize that just because I cannot see any inconsistencies in this narrative, it's no guarantee that others will not. This booklet is offered with the hope that others more capable and experienced than its writer will freely offer their judgment.

The response of Barker and others who have spread the Easter Challenge will be interesting to watch. I'd still like Nielsen to pay his promised thousand dollar reward, as a matter of principle as much as anything else. At a minimum I hope the critics will stop accusing the resurrection accounts of contradiction; but even more so, I hope they'll reconsider their appraisal of the claim of the resurrection itself. The narrative of the life of Jesus is consistent with the Old Testament promises and prophecies of his arrival and mission; and the narrative of his resurrection is consistent with the historical evidence that God indeed raised him from the dead. Jesus gave his witnesses infallible direct proof that he was alive following his passion. Those eyewitnesses were so convinced that many committed their lives to the spreading of his gospel and making disciples of all nations.

The Gospels and other New Testament books were written in the faith community that grew as a result of the testimony of the original eyewitnesses. They must have read the Gospels and helped circulate them—that fact offers assurance that in the minds of the witnesses, the documents provided an accurate portrayal of the events they saw and experienced.

A dead man coming back to life is a grand thing to claim. Were it possible to prove the resurrection accounts contradictory as skeptics have asserted, such a thing might give some a reason to justify their doubt. But what now? Like a phone that won't stop ringing, we must all answer, and will answer the question: Did Jesus literally rise from the dead?

According to the gospel message found in Scripture, God gave Jesus as an offering to save us from the eternal consequence of our sin and to free us from death by his own death. That we can know Jesus of Nazareth was indeed the promised Messiah of the Old Testament and that he succeeded in obtaining our redemption, God offers us the sign of his resurrection from the dead. Study the evidence of this sign for yourself. You might find it more convincing than the critics have claimed. If the evidence wins your thoughts, God may win your heart.

Does this book succeed in presenting the resurrection accounts consistently, without contradiction? You might want to judge it by the same criteria I used in developing it. (1) Is it true to exactly what the Scripture says? (2) Does it require the meaning of words to be altered to make them fit the narrative? (3) Is it logical? Meaning, with the exception of obviously supernatural claims, does it fit within the natural timeline of the characters doing what could be naturally expected of them?

Not everything in the Bible is logical, far from it. Spiritual things are above-logic and the Bible has multiple truth claims which are impossible to falsify. We're challenged to accept them, or reject them. But if we're to believe the Bible's heavenly things, its earthly things need to make sense and pass the test of plausibility.

For my part, I believe the resurrection accounts show that God gave the most important narrative in the Bible with such complexity as to imprint it with his signature. The potential for contradiction is vast, yet none can be proved. This doesn't rise to the level of absolute proof, but it sets forth the puzzling proof of the Lord's resurrection offered in Scripture in such a way that the truth claims of each account is complemented and supported by the truth claims of the rest. Being brought together as one, the accounts clearly give harmonious voice to the same testimony: Christ is risen indeed.

## AFTERWORD

The Bible's core theological message is simple. It's an epic from the quills of over forty writers through 1,500 years of ancient history; an unfolding story of Eden lost, the promise of a coming Savior, and his victory through death which was ultimately proved by his resurrection. No one can read the Book without looking within to think about themselves in relationship to the story and its history. Scripture is no longer being written, but the story continues. The Bible invites us to join in; to sign-on as one for whom the Savior gave his life. The Bible's infinite boundless God who sunk himself into human flesh to die for mankind would have died to save just you. It's difficult to imagine that we have been so loved, but it's true.

We've all heard of the crime of identity theft. That's what Jesus did, but in reverse. Without your permission he assumed your identity and stepped into your personal business between you and God. He took your place. He took control of your account as if it were his own; not to add to your debt like a thief, but to pay your debt like a friend. Justice demands payment for sin, and according to the high law of heaven, your debt has been paid in full. It's already done. God only asks for you to acknowledge that the debt exists, that you've sinned in violation of his law, and that you accept him on his terms: simple faith.

> For God so loved the world, that He gave His only begotten Son, that whoever believes in Him shall not perish, but have eternal life. (John 3:16)

God asks us to trust him because faith is central to every relationship. You know how it works. In good faith we get along well with one another, in bad faith we separate. The same is true with God. He acted in good faith in creation, giving us life. We acted in bad faith by sin. And he acted in good faith in giving Christ so our eternal relationship with him could be put back in good standing. That's the good news. It's simple. His gift is ours by faith.

As a fellow-citizen of earth with you, and a small town pastor who has prayerfully thought about these things long and hard, it seems to me that we are trapped between two worlds, heaven and hell. Life is sometimes heavenly and sometimes hellish. This can't be by accident. I think the whole thing can be reduced to God's quest to be known and loved. He wants the very same thing we all want. The holy angels of heaven love and worship God, but their praise is different in comparison to our own. We've experienced something they haven't; we were lost, enslaved to sin, bound to death and darkness, *and then saved*. It's a great, great story. One supported by more than enough evidence to easily believe, IF you want to. But, just the same, if you don't want to believe, the evidence falls short of qualifying as absolute proof; it is not so convincing as to be undeniable. It's just what God meant it to be.

Whether you consider yourself a Christian, an agnostic, or an atheist, or something else ... don't follow the herd. Even if you're in a church, don't think you're on solid ground just by having membership. Heaven and hell are far too consequential, and lasting, not to find time and solitude to reason the matter through. Do your own thinking and seeking.

There's something called New Atheism emerging. It is atheism pumped full of bravado. It is not only fiercely opposed to religion, but even opposed to the idea that religion should be tolerated by society in any form. In this spirit, atheists, skeptics, and agnostics have accused the Bible's most critically important story of contradiction. Some have said it is so riddled with inconsistencies that only the hopelessly credulous (those foolish enough to believe anything) could possibly believe the resurrection was a real historical event. It seems that in their hatred for anything Christian, they reached too far. They never imagined such a case as the one you hold in your hand would ever be made.

God is full of surprises.

# ENDNOTES

[1] The Prometheus Society, retrieved November 05, 2008, <http://www.prometheussociety.org/>

[2] Nielsen, Ralph. *The Lewiston Morning Tribune*, Lewiston, Idaho, Letters to the Editor, April 21, 2003.

[3] Due to a lack of response, Nielsen quit paying the rent for the PO Box he originally supplied in his Easter Challenge. That's why I removed the PO Box. To the best of my knowledge, Nielsen is still replying to the email address provided.

[4] Till, Farrell. "The Resurrection Maze," *The Skeptical Review,* March-April, 1992, http://www.theskepticalreview.com/tsrmag/2maze92.html. Retrieved for this writing November 6, 2008.

[5] Tremblay, Francois. "The Easter Challenge," *Suite 101.* www.suite101.com/article.cfm/atheism/95672, retrieved July 01, 2008.

[6] See Mt. 16:21, Mt. 17:23, Mt. 20:19, Mt. 27:64, Mk. 9:31, Mk. 10:34, Lk. 9:22, Lk. 13:32, Lk. 18:33, Lk. 24:7, Lk. 24: 46, Jn. 2:1, Acts 10:40, Acts 27:19, and 1 Co. 15:4.

[7] Habermas, Gary. "Resurrection Research from 1975 to the Present," *Journal for the Study of the Historical Jesus*, 3.2, 2005. pp. 135-153